ENNEAGRAM 2

A Spirituality of Brokenness

by

Éilís Bergin PBVM
and
Eddie Fitzgerald SDB

Cover Art: H. Grabowski

Designed, published and distributed by:

SDB MEDIA, Salesian College, Celbridge, Co. Kildare
Tel: (01) 627 5060 Fax: (01) 630 3601
E-mail: sdbmedia@eircom.net
Web: http://homepage.eircom.net/~sdbmedia

Healing our Brokenness

Broken people are beautiful. There is something about vulnerability, suffering and pain that the human heart responds to, instinctively. We become sympathetic, tender, warm and protective towards those whose wounds show through their skin. It doesn't matter whether these wounds are physical, psychological or spiritual. Brokenness in all its forms cries out to be healed. Our wounds speak louder than our words ever could.

The cry of the broken-hearted reaches out and doesn't stop until it finds God, who holds all things in being. The Christian message is that, in Jesus, God has sent his own Son to become truly human, to share our brokenness. In doing so he revealed to us that we are all broken people, whether we know it or not.

There are so many ways in which we are broken. When we are neglected and left alone, something inside us is torn. When we are physically, emotionally or sexually abused, something inside us snaps. When we feel unwanted or betrayed, our heart is wounded. When we experience empty promises and religious doubts, our spirits falter. When we are burdened with shame and tortured with guilt, the pain is always there. When we taste depression and are filled with fear, we find ourselves being ripped asunder. When we no longer find sense or meaning in our lives, we reach the depths of despair.

The central core of the gospel story is that, no matter how broken we are, we are all beautiful and we are all loved. Regardless of what scars we carry, we are loved with an incredible intensity by God. This love is shown in the way Jesus healed the sick, the blind, the deaf, the lame, the lepers, the bereaved, the possessed - the entire company of walking wounded whose hurt called forth such a tender response. This love is expressed in its starkest form in a bruised, battered body nailed to a wooden cross. To be broken is not something irreparable. In the death and resurrection of Christ our wounds have been bound up and healed.

One of the most important things that the Enneagram

tells us is that we are all different, that we all have characteristic and appropriate ways of doing things which are fundamentally related to our particular outlook, to the driving force
of our lives. Each one of us sees reality from a different perspective. We don't stand in each other's shoes, but make our
own distinctive footprints on the path of life.

It follows, therefore, that we do not all go to God in the
same way, that there is no one path to holiness and, consequently, no one 'right' way to pray. In terms of the Enneagram our approach to God will be at one with the centre of
our basic energy, whether that be our heart, our head or our
gut. We pray and go to God as we are, not as we are not.

This little book is addressed to those who have already
some basic knowledge of the Enneagram. It is an attempt to
meet the needs of those people who say: "I know where I am
on the Enneagram, but where do I go from here? How does it
help me on my spiritual journey?"

Before we started to write, we asked many people what
they thought was needed. In essence they suggested three
things. It needs to be short - people don't want verbiage, they
want to be able to focus their attention, not to have it dif-
fused. It needs to be simple - they don't want complicated
jargon. And, most of all, it needs to be real - to be honest,
sincere and grounded in lived experience.

Spirituality is the way we respond to the presence of God
in our lives. St. Irenaeus of Lyons had a beautifully perceptive insight into the significance of the Incarnation. He said:
"What is not accepted is not redeemed." Because we whole-
heartedly agree with this, we have chosen here to follow a
very simple procedure. The first step is to identify our core
sin, to *name it* in all its stark reality. Having done so, we then
claim it as our own, acknowledging its specific dominance in
our lives. Finally, we learn to *tame it*, especially by means of
the help obtained through scriptural meditation and prayer.

Most of us are put off by books on spirituality with
grandiose titles. But we can all identify with the notion of
brokenness because we have all been wounded by life, we all
have our inner place of pain. We can relate with broken people because we know that vulnerability is part of the fallen
human condition, that we are not angels but embodied spirits. This is what it means to take our humanity seriously.

On a personal note, the authors have each seen children
and adults who have been wounded and hurt by others,

sometimes even by those who were supposed to have been their healers. At home and abroad, at work and in counselling situations, looking into our hearts and sharing our own stories, we have come to realize the ache within us all.

In our own lives, both of us have experienced physical, emotional, psychological and spiritual brokenness. We consider this to be a blessing, because it has made us realize the need we have for the healing power of God's love.

The Enneagram, after all, is only a tool. Of itself it has no power to save. For us, as Christians, Christ is the one who saves. But one of the great strengths of the Enneagram is that it allows us to see clearly the hidden source of our individual brokenness and increases our compassion for the pain this brings. It is a powerful tool for showing us the shadow side of our personality - our compulsions, our addictions, our dysfunctional patterns of behaviour and, above all, our hidden sin.

The core sins really are killers because frequently we don't even know or acknowledge that they are ours. We admit to many faults but *not* to our central, most deadly one. "That's not me at all," we say. But it is. The problem is that very often we don't see what others see, because we are so successful at keeping it hidden from ourselves. We have many ways of escaping our inner pain. We are endlessly creative at devising defence mechanisms to protect us from our central compulsion.

In our earlier booklet, *"The Enneagram: The Quest for Self Transcendence"*, we concentrated on profiling the nine basic compulsive energies which drive us. Now we concentrate on how we can grow in and through our brokenness. This will take time and is not going to be easy. In the spiritual life, too, there is no such thing as a free lunch. We generally get what we pay for. But it is our belief that we will also get what we pray for.

On our spiritual journey towards conversion we can be as imaginative and inventive as we like. What's important is that we begin. It's amazing how differently we think about things when we pray about them. Prayer helps us see things from God's perspective. In the process we develop a whole new way of looking at the world. This in turn, gradually leads to a radical change of heart. Our prayer is that we will all experience the healing power of God's love.

ONES

DAILY PRAYER

Lord God, I thank you for giving me
a keen sense of what is right
and a diligent desire to do good.
In my attempts to live up to my ideals,
help me to be patient and forgiving.
Teach me to be tolerant of mistakes
rather than always finding fault with things.
Show me how to accept what is good enough
and, above all, how to lighten up,
enjoy life and gently relax in your love.

Amen.

Name It:

My Name:	The Perfectionist
My Vice:	Anger
My God:	The All-Perfect, Just Judge
My Masks:	Resentment, Anxiety, Rigidity, Jealousy
My Need:	Patience
My Virtue:	Serenity

Claim It:

Deep down I'm very angry. That's my brokenness. I don't normally admit this. I generally cover it up so that nobody knows. But the tenseness of my body, in particular my face, often betrays me. I have a very strong sense of right and wrong and an inner voice criticizes me when I fail. I don't want to be seen as a hypocrite. I do so want to measure up to what God expects of me. The trouble is that I also want to achieve the impossibly high standards I frequently set for myself. And because I don't, I am fundamentally angry - at God for not creating me perfect in the first place, at others for contributing to the mess the world is in, and at myself for not arriving more rapidly at what I consider to be spiritual wholeness. Time just runs away from me and I think I'll never make it.

I always want to live from strength, not weakness. So a spirituality of self-control rather than of brokenness is much more my style. I dislike the cold shell I have constructed because it makes it difficult for others to get to know me, and gives the impression that I am dismissive of people. In reality, though, it is only a way of protecting myself from getting hurt and from letting others see that I bleed too.

Other people seem to have a much easier life and I resent that. Because I see so clearly the faults in everything and everyone, I have become judgemental, critical and negative. Only grudgingly and with deliberate effort am I a source of affirmation and praise. I often think that when I share what little goodness I have, I somehow diminish my own store of it.

Lord God, there are times when I look at myself and see only a sinner and you as a Just Judge who will make me pay for all my imperfections. I know that both of these are inadequate and that in reality you are wonderfully compassionate and I am fundamentally good. I just need to be patient, to do what I can and then to wait for the growth which comes through your healing touch.

Tame It:
Allowing God to work in us, to heal our anger and ease our pain is a life-long process. We mustn't be impatient or want everything 'now'. A spirituality which is strongly influenced by social justice issues is attractive to our type, given our interest in putting things right and transforming the mess.

However, the quiet, gentle approach is often what we need most. This is all the more important since we experience the world as being bigger than we are. It follows that we feel we have to work harder to control our environment and set things right. When we let God be God and not take on ourselves the burden of single-handedly trying to improve on creation, we will save ourselves a lot of needless anxiety.

The following suggestions for reflection and prayer, though not exhaustive, may help.

■ *Matthew 10:1-16 (The workers in the vineyard)*
This parable makes us face up to the reality that life is not about fairness, but about gift. We are invited to become co-workers in building the Kingdom. But God's generosity is

always unconditional and does not depend on our effort. Still less does it depend on keeping lists of rules and regulations, like the Pharisees to whom it was originally addressed.

■ *Luke 15:11-32 (The parable of the prodigal son)*
Reflecting on the role of the elder, dutiful son in this parable brings us face to face with our own moralistic self-righteousness. Like him, our spiritual hit-list may well include members of our own family. While we make every effort to contain our anger, it generally comes out in the form of resentment. The model Jesus offers us is that of the compassionate father.

■ *Luke 6:41-42 (On not being so judgemental)*
Our over-ready ability to see the faults in others often blinds us to similar faults in ourselves. Sometimes we miss the wood for the trees. Tolerance of mistakes and a willingness to learn are gospel values worth cultivating.

■ *Mark 12:31 (Self-love is a condition for loving others)*
In general we are far too hard on ourselves. We never let up. Jesus teaches us that we are fundamentally good rather than flawed. We cannot love others unless we first love ourselves.

■ *Matthew 13:24-30 (Waiting for growth)*
We find it difficult to tolerate imperfection and ambiguity, so we are frequently seduced by the urgency of our desire for clean-cut immediate solutions. But real life is messy. We need to trust God and be patient with ourselves and others.

PRACTICAL SUGGESTION

◊◊◊ *We are high-energy people who are relentless in our pursuit of justice, right and moral perfection. What we need is to experience the peace and tranquillity of being quiet in God's presence. It helps to find a comfortable posture and relax tense muscles. An icon or other symbol may prove useful to get us started. There is no need for us to worry about putting words to our prayer. Since time is so important to us, having a set time for prayer each day helps. What we are trying to foster is receptivity and the generosity of 'letting go'. This will make it easier to forget our cares, concerns and current involvements and assist in calming our restless analytical minds.*

TWOS

DAILY PRAYER

Lord God, I thank you for giving me
the gift of a generous heart.
Help me to understand that
your love for me does not depend
on what I do for other people.
Show me how to minister to
the needs of others
without losing sight of my own.
Allow me to feel in my own wounds
the healing power of your love.

Amen.

Name It:

My Name:	The Helper
My Vice:	Pride
My God:	The Eternal Caregiver
My Masks:	Flattery, Privilege, Ambition, Seduction
My Need:	Acceptance of real worth
My Virtue:	Humility

Claim It:

Deep down I'm proud. That's my brokenness. I feel I'm better than others because I'm generally more caring. I see the needs of others even before they do themselves and do everything I can to help them, sometimes without even being asked. I constantly put myself out to be of service, but I also expect people to recognize and appreciate what I do for them.

However, when I really think about it, I know that my helpfulness is both a source of recognition and a way of seeing myself as being of value. I know that what appears to others as selfless and generous is not entirely so. There are often strings attached. I exercise pressure indirectly and by stealth.

I don't blatantly seek to manipulate, but I know that what I do is manipulative nonetheless. Being helpful is my way of getting attention, of asking for love without putting it into words. It feels good to have people who depend on me. Their need gives me a sense of being important, useful and worthwhile. It helps define who I am.

Lord God, I know this means I don't have a good self-image, and that I don't appreciate the gift you have given me. You love me unconditionally. I don't have to keep proving myself, to you or to anyone else. I don't have to try so hard to please all the time. Love cannot be earned or paid for. It is always a gift. Help me to realize that the needs I perceive in others are often a reflection of those within myself. Give me the humility to accept that I, too, am in need of help.

Tame It:
Our constant concern for others frequently masks the lack of attention we pay to our own physical, emotional, psychological and spiritual needs. We help others and neglect ourselves. But if we're always giving, always active, is there anything for ourselves when at some point we stop the treadmill? Who fills the emptiness of our personal storehouse?

We need to learn the spiritual truth that 'charity begins at home', that without a realistic acceptance of our own woundedness, we cannot even begin to understand the pain of others let alone help them alleviate it. We have to learn to make the journey inward. In doing so, since we have lived so long with our need to be needed, we shouldn't be surprised to find ourselves acting out of it, even when we've made significant efforts to counter its grip. We need the humility to accept our brokenness and the patience to allow God's love to heal our wounds.

The following suggestions for reflection and prayer, though not exhaustive, may help.

■ *Luke 10:38-42 (Martha and Mary)*
In God's presence everything is placed in its proper perspective. Mary is praised because she allows the Lord to minister to her needs before she ministers to those of others. God has no need of the martyr complex. Martha manipulatively tries to get Jesus on her side and urges him to proclaim the importance of service. Instead, she learns that this is but one value among others. Hospitality, duty and task-sharing are

12

undoubtedly important, but only one thing is essential.

■ *Mark 12:31 (Love others as you love yourself)*
It is important to put first things first. Charity begins at home for the good reason that if we are not loving towards ourselves we cannot possibly be loving towards others. Care, compassion and respect for the self are essential prerequisites for extending them to others.

■ *Mark 10:35-44 (A lesson in humility)*
James and John let their pride run away with them. They were prepared to suffer anything provided they got the highest places in the Kingdom. But Jesus reminds us all that genuine service is not a power-play. When we look for preferment we are effectively attached to a false self-image, one which is fundamentally empty and in need of shoring up.

■ *Mark 14:32-42 (Facing our inner fears)*
Jesus was no stranger to feelings. In Gethsemane he experienced inner distress and great fear. He shared these feelings with his friends and wasn't ashamed to ask for their help. Indeed, his loneliness was compounded by their weakness.

■ *Luke 4:42-44 (The right to say 'No')*
We need to give proper time to our own spiritual needs and not allow our compulsive generosity to rule our lives. Saying 'No' to others should not make us feel guilty. They have no right to the last drop.

PRACTICAL SUGGESTION

◊◊◊ *Since we undervalue our own needs it is important to find a place (in a family, community or among friends) where we, too, are looked after. But we also need to make a space in our day for ourselves alone. During this time it is vital to concentrate on being rather than on doing. First we need to relax. Aromatherapy may help, or listening to some soothing meditative music. However, this is but a preparation for our doing some serious inner work. We have to face our own wounds, our own neediness - the personal concerns we regularly set aside for the sake of ministering to others. Having named one, we can pray about it and offer it to God for healing.*

13

THREES

DAILY PRAYER

Lord God, I thank you for creating me
in your image and for blessing me
with the drive and energy to succeed.
Help me to realize that
achievement isn't everything,
and that failure can often provide
more truth than success.
Show me how to get beneath
the surface images I love to create
to the even more beautiful centre within.

Amen.

Name It:

My Name:	The Achiever
My Vice:	Deceit
My God:	The Successful Creator
My Masks:	Vanity, Security, Prestige, Ideal Image
My Need:	Examine the Image
My Virtue:	Truth

Claim It:

Deep down I'm deceitful. That's my brokenness. I cover it up so that it's even hidden from myself. I'm radically out of touch with my innermost depths of feeling and love. I keep myself constantly busy so as not to have to face my real self. I am skilled at covering up, at showing a different face for every possible occasion. Pretence comes naturally to me, as I strive to be a winner in everything I do.

I court success, security and prestige because I'm afraid of failure. I don't stop long enough to face the truth behind the masks of my own making. I know I need to learn the success of apparent failure and the failure of what sometimes looks like success. I need to absorb the lesson of the cross, the glory of failure, the economy of grace.

I'm ever restless, always on the move, never still. I prefer to be a moving target rather than a sitting duck. I give the impression that I have it made, that everything comes so easily to me. But in reality, I'm living a lie.

Lord God, there are times when I see myself as a superficial shell, and you as the Successful Creator with whom I long to compete. I know that neither of these is the whole truth. You created me in your image, yet I have spent much of my life trying to embellish it to my own liking, hiding your beautiful handiwork under a constant series of masks.

I know you love me in spite of my duplicity and image-making. You are interested in the reality not in the substitute image. You see the human vulnerable face behind my high-profile, self-sufficient mask. Help me to get in touch with my need for others, with the tender side of my heart and with the truth beyond the soft option and the hard sell.

Show me that what I achieve in worldly terms is as nothing to the generosity of your passionate love. My life is lived at a frenetic pace, but you see the still centre where my heart aches and I crave for love. Slow me down, Lord, so that I can with calm heart know the real secret of creative love.

Tame It:
Risking the self-revelation and self-giving of love takes time. Our defences have been built up over many years. Deceit is not healed in a day. The failures we experience as we grow in a spirituality of radical truthfulness should be an encouragement to us that we are moving in the direction of wholeness. For us the movement is from the external to the internal. What we *do* is undoubtedly important, but what we *are* is vital. Like all other personality types we have to keep a proper balance between *being* and *doing*.

The following suggestions for reflection and prayer, though not exhaustive, may help.

■ *John 8:32 (The truth will set us free)*
Our constant movement may seduce us into thinking that we are genuinely free spirits. However, true freedom consists not in running away, but in standing one's ground. It is not pretence but honesty. Truth, not the sophisticated veneer of self-deception, is what will make us free.

- **Luke 9:46-48** *(Who is the greatest in the Kingdom?)*
Position, prestige and privilege cut no ice with Jesus. Our emphasis on the significant roles we play does not impress him. What does get through is a childlike heart - the ability to live life without duplicity.

- **Luke 18:9-14** *(The Pharisee and the Publican)*
Never mind the quality, feel the width! We are well able to show off, to boast about our achievements, to imagine that once we have successfully managed our image we have some-how made it. But God is not impressed by the vanity of self-advertisement. If we pray like that we will end up like the Pharisee - talking to ourselves.

- **John 6:63-71** *(The loyalty of the true follower)*
When we truly believe, we must be prepared to be faithful. We have difficulty with that. We are inclined to abandon projects in mid-stream if there is a danger that their failure will tarnish our image. We need reminding that if we don't stand for some-thing, we are in danger of falling for anything.

- **John 15:13-17** *(Love is the key)*
God judges us on the quality of our love, not on who we know or what our qualifications are. We need friendship in our lives. We need to see God as a loving friend, who knows our weak-ness and chooses us regardless. We are called to go beyond the exterior in our dealings with others, so that our love is both true and sincere.

PRACTICAL SUGGESTION

◊◊◊ *Since we tend to be out of touch with our emotions it is important to tap this source of energy in prayer. Generally we find that our emotions slow us down and don't allow us to be as productive and efficient as we want to be. But prayer is more about presence than productivity, about wasting time cre-atively rather than having something to show for it. Far from being boring, such time-wasting can prove to be deeply energiz-ing. Using music and posture to introduce us to the stillness of our centre can be very helpful. Also, since movement is one of our strengths, why not harness it in our prayer? Dance, drama or simple repetitive movement may be useful here.*

FOURS

DAILY PRAYER

Lord God, I thank you for giving me
a keen eye for beauty and
a special sensitivity to the human heart.
Show me how even the most ordinary
and everyday realities are filled
with the wonder of your presence.
Help me to live in the present moment
and to appreciate that my
tears and laughter, joy and pain,
are part of your loving plan for the world.
                                        Amen.

Name It:

My Name:	The Artist
My Vice:	Envy
My God:	Sensitive Creator of Beauty
My Masks:	Melancholy, Resistance, Shame, Competition
My Need:	Sense of present reality
My Virtue:	Equanimity (Harmony)

Claim It:

Deep down I'm envious. That's my brokenness. I'm usually too ashamed or too caught up in my own feelings to admit this. I'm so afraid of the pain of rejection. I long to be special, to be different, somehow to rise above the ordinary and the mundane. I am especially sensitive to beauty in all its forms. I love anything which is simple, natural, authentic. My standards are so high that the more I try to reach them, the more artificial I become. I can't help comparing myself with people who have more talent, taste, sophistication and class than I have and longing to be somehow superior.

I envy them the ease with which they seem to live their

17

lives. It's easier for me to live in memories, dreams and the world of the arts than in the everyday world, where the mess is part of the reality. I have real problems with intimacy and distance. What I have, I don't value; what I long for, I treasure. I'm regularly disappointed by life and this makes me sad. Why is it that others seem to have it all? Even in my relationships I'm jealous of others being somehow more interesting or attractive than I am. I'm ashamed of my body, my inner turmoil disgusts me and I regularly run myself down. Is it any wonder that I have a poor self-image?

Lord God, all of this causes me intense inner suffering. I go through a roller-coaster of feelings, from ecstatic joy to inexpressible sadness. People think this is just moodiness. If only they knew how deep it goes, they'd see what a dreadful burden it is.

Life is such a struggle for me, Lord, yet I'm tragically unwilling to accept help. Please help me. Help me to appreciate the special sensitivity and intuition you have given me - the ability to understand at depth the emotional life of others. Show me how to be realistic enough not to imagine this world as the safe haven of my dreams, but as holding in balance tears and laughter, pain and joy, ugliness and beauty, violence and peace. Help me not to be so elitist, so snobbish, but to value the normal, the ordinary and the everyday.

Tame It:

For us the movement is from the romanticized memories of the past and the hoped-for visions of the future to the humdrum reality of the present. We need to learn to be at ease and content with the way things are, understanding that "God is in the pots and pans" (Teresa of Avila), that we meet God in the ordinary, the everyday, the mundane, the pedestrian, the hackneyed. Rather than bemoan people's misunderstanding of who we are, we should try to use our talents for drama, ritual, art, music, poetry and symbol to give a powerful voice to those who cannot speak as eloquently or protest as imaginatively as we can. But we must not be surprised if it takes time for us to readjust our priorities in this way.

The following suggestions for reflection and prayer, though not exhaustive, may help.

■   *Matthew 6:25-34 (Everything is in God's hands)*
Nothing is ordinary in God's sight. Even the birds of the air

and the grass in the fields take on a numinous significance, an eternal aspect which reflects the tender care of the Creator. We are no less special or cared for than they. The ordinary is energizing when seen in this light, and distinctions between sacred and secular disappear.

■   *Matthew 18:23-35   (The unforgiving steward)*
Jesus tells us that when we are consumed with our own self-interest we lose our sense of proportion, our compassion and our sensitivity to others.

■   *Mark 10:13-16   (Like little children)*
Children are still open to the wonder of life. They have not lost their delight in the everyday. Familiarity has not yet led them to contempt. They see the beauty of things with innocent eyes and listen to their truth with a welcoming heart.

■   *John 19:1-11 . (Being crowned with thorns)*
Jesus experienced abandonment and rejection in dramatic fashion towards the end of his life. But, however humiliated, he relied on God's help and placed himself in God's care.

■   *John 2:1-12   (The wedding at Cana)*
Everyday elements (water and wine) combined with a discerning heart can transform impending disasters into celebrations of joy. Like Jesus and Mary we can bring happiness to others by our sensitivity to their needs.

PRACTICAL SUGGESTION

◊◊◊   *Our tendency is to live on the inside and over-emphasize our feelings. But, if we are to grow spiritually, it is vital that we learn to get our feelings in perspective, and get some balance into the relationship between our inner life and the messy reality around us. Yoga, massage or aromatherapy may help us relax and become less intense. Journaling (keeping a record of what's happening in our lives) may help us distance ourselves from our feelings, and is a useful safety-valve for externalizing our inner concerns. Since relationships are very important to us, shared prayer and liturgy, and getting involved in social justice issues, can be especially meaningful and life-giving.*

FIVES

DAILY PRAYER

Lord God. I thank you for giving me
an enquiring mind
and the gift of discernment.
Help me to reach out more to people,
and to trust the wisdom
that comes from the heart.
Give me the generosity
to share my insights with those I meet,
and the courage to involve myself
in their daily cares and concerns.

Amen.

Name It:

My Name: The Observer
My Vice: Avarice / Greed
My God: The Ultimate Source of Meaning
My Masks: Stinginess, Withdrawal, Guru, Confidence
My Need: To get involved
My Virtue: Detachment

Claim It:

Deep down I'm greedy and avaricious, not so much for material things as for the knowledge that will give my life meaning. That's my brokenness. I find it hard to admit this, even to myself, and I have the skills to cover it up so that nobody knows. But the truth is that I'm so afraid of feeling empty inside that I continually long for fulfilment. I dread the idea of meaninglessness and my continual quest for knowledge is simply my way of dealing with this.

Sometimes I experience such great loneliness that the only way I can feel safe is to shut myself away, most frequently by living inside my head. I appear confident and self-assured on the surface, but deep down I experience a great deal of insecurity. I attempt to fill the void by my passion for collecting and hoarding. I don't like intrusions and am very protective of my own space.

I generally try to remain calm and keep my emotions under control. When I'm angry, upset, fearful or emotional, I try not to show it. But I do feel things deeply. It's just that I tend to analyse my feelings rather than immediately experience them. I find it hard to express my emotions or put them into words. It's much easier for me to show warmth towards friends who are absent rather than those who are present.

Lord God, you know me better than I do myself. You know how difficult it is for me to trust other people, to let go of my 'fortress mentality', to avoid being cynical. I consider myself superior to others because I think I'm perceptive enough to see through their superficiality and sham. But the loss is mine, not theirs. I've lost the common touch because of my tendency to over-analyse everything.

Lord, I know I'm not the 'giving' sort. I certainly find it very painful to get involved. I both long for and somehow feel threatened by intimacy. I don't look for attention and don't allow others the opportunity for making demands on me. I limit my contacts with people and compartmentalize my life precisely in order to avoid involvement. I prefer to retreat or intellectualize rather than get 'stuck in'.

Tame It:
Our spiritual journey is from the internal to the external. It involves taking the incarnation seriously. It means accepting that knowledge comes through the heart and the senses as well as through the head. The fact is that God became flesh, not newsprint, and there's no escaping the implications of that. Unfortunately, there is a painful split within us between theory and practice, between contemplation and action. We must be bold enough to risk involvement, and inventive enough to give practical expression to our insights and reflections. Then we will not give in to disengagement and others will be able to share in the wisdom we have to offer.

The following suggestions for reflection and prayer, though not exhaustive, may help.

■ *John 9:39-41 (Those with sight can be blind to the truth)*
There is a difference between knowledge and wisdom, between

sight and insight. What we think we know can blind us to other possibilities and prevent us from learning from the poor and needy who stand in front of our eyes.

■ *Luke 10:29-37 (The Good Samaritan)*
It is very easy to theorize and generalize about what needs to be done to provide a solution to people's problems. Non-involvement is a form of opting out, of passing by 'on the other side'. Jesus demands that we give flesh to our beliefs and discover the truths that only touching the wounds can bring.

■ *Luke 6:38 (We receive in the measure that we give)*
Our unwillingness to risk sharing what we have with a generous heart frequently prevents us from receiving more ourselves. If we hoard what we have and are stingy with our gifts, we are unlikely to be open enough to receive the unexpected.

■ *John 11:32-44 (Jesus is moved to tears)*
We don't really trust our feelings. We find it hard to express emotion, to show how deeply we care for others. This gospel story shows how Jesus expresses his love unashamedly and does something constructive about it.

■ *Luke 11:9-13 (Ask and you will receive)*
It is difficult for us to ask for help to meet our needs or fill the empty place within our hearts. We much prefer to go it alone and make do. But God is the generous giver, whose compassionate presence brings love and meaning into our lives.

PRACTICAL SUGGESTION

◊◊◊ *Since we tend to over-emphasize the mind and are open to a wide variety of prayer options, it is important for us to anchor our thoughts and get in touch with our heart. We can often best do this by concentrating on some symbol - a lighted candle, a cake of bread, a mantra etc. - which will help us centre our thoughts and not allow them to jump about in a free-fall meditation. Our body is very important in prayer, so posture, breathing, clothing, warmth and so on are particularly relevant. All of these can keep us open to the promptings of the real world when we place ourselves in God's presence. In this way there will always be an active element in our contemplation.*

SIXES

DAILY PRAYER

Lord God, I thank you for giving me
a great respect for the law and
the gift of loyalty to friends.
Help me to understand more deeply
how much you really love me.
Safe in the knowledge of this love
and relying on your tender care,
may I have the courage to
overcome my fears and become
more trusting of myself and others.

Amen.

Name It:

My Name:	The Supporter
My Vice:	Fear / Anxiety
My God:	Ultimate Security
My Masks:	Doubt, Warmth, Obedience, Hard/Soft
My Need:	Faith
My Virtue:	Courage

Claim It:

Deep down I'm full of fear. That's my brokenness. I'm not willing to admit it, but it comes out in my doubts and in my deeply anxious approach to life. I am very mistrustful - of myself and others. I seem to be continually watchful and afraid. My self-doubt and lack of self-confidence makes me much too dependent on others, particularly on those in a position of authority. Relying on tradition, the law and the institutions of society gives me a great sense of security and helps allay my fear of making a mistake.

I find it difficult to trust my own abilities and instincts. Yet, at the same time, I do not completely trust others. I can spot danger a mile off and am quick to look for cover. I prefer to see things in straightforward terms, in black and white rather than shades of grey. I like to be sure of my position and not contradict myself. To do so, I pay attention to detail. The trouble is that I then find it hard to make up my mind. I either hesitate and allow myself to be led by others, or I over-compensate, become obstinate, defiant and take risks.

Even though I work well in a group, the model I work out of is hierarchical. There is a sense in which my loyalty to the group is just an expression of my basic insecurity - a way of finding strength in numbers. I don't really have the courage of my own convictions. Indeed, my sense of duty is often a cover for my anxiety about making decisions for myself. What it amounts to is a fear of freedom, a fundamental unwillingness to say 'yes' or 'no' on my own.

Lord God, what I need is faith in you and in my own goodness. I find it difficult to accept undiluted praise because I don't really believe in my own value and worth. But you have given me a wonderful variety of talents and gifts, and called me into your close circle of friends.

Help me to realize, Lord, that you do not expect impossible standards from me. Give me the faith to believe that you love me for who I am. Give me the courage to take responsibility for my day-to-day choices. Help me to give myself permission to own my feelings and to open myself up to you and others in a relationship of mutual trust and intimacy.

Tame It:
Our spiritual journey is from the inside out, from self-protective assessment to courageous commitment. We have to venture forth and risk the possibility of getting shot down. We cannot keep backing out of life, refusing to make decisions or get involved for fear of what might go wrong. We have a 'stop-go' mentality, an 'on-off' approach. If we wait until we have certitude we will never act at all. True discipleship involves costly action. Trust in God means facing our fear of the unfamiliar, the unknown and the unexpected.

The following suggestions for reflection and prayer, though not exhaustive, may help.

■ *Matthew 25:14-30 (Parable of the talents)*
This parable is essentially about seizing the opportunity when it is presented, rather than being so cautious that we allow

ourselves to be paralysed by fear.

■ *John 20:24-29 (Doubt no more, but believe)*
We like certainties and find it difficult to cope with doubt, ambiguity or loose ends. We are afraid to risk committing ourselves without supporting evidence. Our search for verification can even lead us to withdraw from others and in so doing miss the unexpected truth. But God is patient with us and gently leads us to inner conviction and faith.

■ *Mark 2:23-28 (The sabbath is made for man)*
Jesus respected the law, but was not limited by it. He had the inner freedom to act beyond the social, cultural and religious boundaries of his time. In doing so he was able to reach everyone - tax-collectors, prostitutes, lepers and, even, gentiles.

■ *John 15:9-17 (God loves us deeply)*
Fear results from over-exaggerating what is expected of us. When we deepen our awareness of God's love for us, we begin to experience an inner confidence without which we can have no lasting security. Moreover, we can then learn to re-direct the energies we vainly spend in trying to counter our fears.

■ *Matthew 10:26-33 (The courage of our convictions)*
With God's protection and providence there is no need to be afraid. Understanding that enables us to be courageous in professing our faith and witnessing to the truth, no matter how intimidating the circumstances may be.

PRACTICAL SUGGESTION

◊◊◊ *As a rule we tend to keep our guard up and are afraid to let go. We don't trust our feelings and avoid spontaneity. It will help us in our prayer if we do what we can to trust our deepest selves and continually remind ourselves that God loves us. Talking with God as we would to a best friend will move us on from repeating set formulas written by others. If we focus on our breathing, we can make each breath a 'thank-you' to the Spirit, the Breath of Life. Another suggestion is to place our hands palms upwards on our knees and, with our eyes fixed on them, allow them to reflect back to us our letting go of fear and our openness to whatever God surprises us with.*

SEVENS

DAILY PRAYER

Lord God, I thank you for giving me
a childlike enthusiasm and the ability
to enjoy the good things in life.
Show me how to embrace everything
with temperance and moderation.
Help me to see that running away
from pain does not lead to happiness.
Give me the wisdom to discover
that joy is to be found, not in the superficial,
but within the depths of my own heart.

Amen.

Name It:

My Name:	The Optimist
My Vice:	Gluttony
My God:	Ultimate Happiness
My Masks:	Planning, Togetherness, Generosity, Fantasy
My Need:	Balance
My Virtue:	Temperance

Claim It:

Deep down I'm intemperate. That's my brokenness. I don't normally admit it, but I'm a glutton for more. What I want is a superabundance of the good things in life, of the things that are likely to bring me happiness. Nothing is ever enough. I consume things rather than savour and enjoy them. I take life in big gulps rather than in little sips. I emphasize the positive and minimize the negative. Basically, what I'm doing is trying to avoid pain and the emptiness inside.

Even though I move around a lot, essentially I live in my head. I'm very idealistic, concentrating on the good and rationalizing or trivializing the difficulties. I have lots of plans and schemes for doing good, but I gloss over the problems. I'm future-orientated, always anticipating life. The fact that I don't fully experience the pleasure of the present leads to my not being completely satisfied. I generally make sure I have so much to do that I'll never get bored. Indeed, my need for constant stimulation leads me, at times, to addictive behaviour.

I look for distractions to keep me occupied and help me cope with painful realities. I find it hard to delay gratification. When I want things I want them now. My senses are so sharp that I can almost taste the enjoyment. The trouble is that I can also vividly imagine the intensity of pain, and I look for every possible diversion to avoid it. That's why I'm continually on the go and try not to get tied down to routine tasks. In effect, I'm running away from myself because I fear that, if I stop to look inside, I won't like what I see.

Lord God, slow me down long enough to discover the depth and beauty within. You have given me a childlike wonder at life, the blessing of good humour and a marvellous sense of fun. I am able to see the ridiculous side of life and make people laugh. That's a precious commodity in today's world. But I need help to realize that I do not have to search for happiness non-stop - that, if I cease my restless pursuit of it, happiness will surely find me. I need to discover that real joy is not dependent on outside circumstances but lies essentially within my own heart. Help me to dig beneath the surface so as to gain the true perspective of depth.

Tame It:
We need to become more reflective and responsible, yet, paradoxically, our spiritual journey is from the inside out. Our natural curiosity and our attraction to constant change and the 'quick fix' make it very difficult for us to focus our attention when we come to pray. There are so many delightful possibilities and options to choose from that, given the opportunity, we attempt to pursue them all. However, we can slow down our mental games by 'anchoring' ourselves in the real. We can do this, for example, by adopting a posture which ensures stillness and stops physical movement. Then we can begin.

The following suggestions for reflection and prayer, though not exhaustive, may help.

■ *Matthew 7:24-27 (Build on rock, not on sand)*
Staying on the surface of life is ultimately doomed to failure.

Real growth and long-term happiness demands a rock-solid foundation of depth. Concentrating on the superficial is no way to build for the future.

■   *Mark 8:31-33* (*Running away is not the answer*)
It is characteristic of us that when the going gets tough we tend to get going! Jesus refuses to throw in the towel when faced with difficulties and disappointments, and sends a clear message to those of us who do.

■   *Matthew 15:21-28* (*Perseverance pays off*)
Our enthusiasm is generally short-lived. But when it comes to difficult life-issues and the healing of brokenness, it is essential to be persistent, to put up with the put-downs and stay with the pain. If we do the chances are that, like the woman in the gospel, we will eventually go away happy.

■   *Mark 12:31* (*Self-love is a condition for loving others*)
We are naturally gregarious. But we shouldn't forget that joy can be found in solitude as well. There is no need for us to fear being on our own. Solitude is not the same as loneliness and inner silence can enrich our understanding of ourselves.

■   *Matthew 14:22-33* (*How to walk on water*)
We find it hard to believe someone will help us when we are in trouble. We have plan B always ready. But God continually surprises us. Even though we are afraid, God's caring presence encourages us to risk getting our feet wet.

PRACTICAL SUGGESTION

◊◊◊ *Since the present doesn't completely satisfy us we are constantly planning for a more enjoyable future and trying to diffuse our pain by over-activity. But it pays off if we learn the art of staying in one place. One way is to sit comfortably with our hands resting gently on our knees, palms up. Instead of closing our eyes and letting the mind have free rein, it is useful to focus on our empty palms, a symbol of our openness to the spirit and of our willingness to let go of our consumer mentality and our materialistic approach to life. Or we could savour the scent of a flower, slowly caress the surface of a leaf, or sit by a lake and feel ourselves part of something greater than ourselves.*

EIGHTS

DAILY PRAYER

Lord God, I thank you for giving me
a tremendous passion for life,
a powerful sense of justice
and the energy to get things done.
Help me always to protect the weak
and champion the oppressed.
Give me a heart filled with compassion
so that I may experience the strength
that comes through gentleness
and the respect that comes through love.
Amen.

Name It:

My Name: The Leader
My Vice: Lust
My God: The Omnipotent Judge
My Masks: Revenge, Control, Friendship, Possession
My Need: Tenderness
My Virtue: Innocence / Childlikeness

Claim It:
Deep down I'm lustful. That's my brokenness. Pleasure for me is bound up with control. I exploit people because of my passion to dominate and possess. I violate their space, use them without shame and humiliate them without guilt. At my worst I simply don't consider how vulnerable people can be and have no respect for their feelings. I satisfy my instincts and enjoy life's pleasures without too many hang-ups. I can be cruel rather than kind. Sometimes I punish people disproportionately for the mistakes that they've made. When I put forward high standards of morality I expect others to live up to them without really feeling obliged to do so myself.

I like to keep tabs on things, to check up on even the most trivial details. It's my way of not letting things get out of hand. I value my independence and prefer to be dominant in my relationships. I'm very possessive and find it hard to compromise or adapt. I tend to bully people and don't respect those who will not fight back. I see things in black and white. People are either for me or against me, friends or enemies.

Without realizing it, I find myself pushing people around. I'm generally insensitive to the hurt I'm causing. I substitute aggressive behaviour for playfulness and sexual activity for intimacy. I have no problem about fighting 'dirty'. I'm direct, often to the point of rudeness, and use strong language to emphasise what I'm trying to say. I don't pull my punches. I say what I mean and mean what I say. I tend to confront rather than communicate. I readily spit out my anger in the belief that attack is the best form of defence.

Lord God, I know you have given me an enormous passion for life, for love and for justice. It comes out in the way I generally take the side of the underdog. But I have to avoid becoming a self-appointed judge and jury, always willing to retaliate when I think the balance needs to be redressed. I have to accept my vulnerability and let others see the tender and more gentle side of me which I keep so well hidden beneath my deliberately tough exterior.

Tame It:
Our inner journey demands an openness to God and to other people. We need to strive to integrate action and contemplation, and to balance passionate expression and a refusal to self-disclose. Since we generally live in the present we find it easy to be immediately present to God in prayer. For us this involves a centring of our selves, an emptying of thoughts and feelings, a letting go of activity and a stillness of loving presence which transcends our everyday wants and needs.

As gut people we naturally want to be doing and are suspicious of inactivity. But our best prayer is that of simple presence. Paradoxically it brings us both a heightened sensitivity and a calming inner tranquillity.

The following suggestions for reflection and prayer, though not exhaustive, may help.

■　*Luke 4:16-23 (Setting the downtrodden free)*
We have been given power so that we can help those who are

powerless. Our strength should be used to help the weak and the marginalized. Our words can speak for those who have no voice and our deeds support those who need protection.

■   *Matthew 14:13-21   (Feeding the hungry)*
The most characteristic gut reaction of Jesus is one of compassion. Whenever people are troubled, harassed, rejected or in difficulty, Jesus doesn't have to think about what to do. Without hesitation he reacts with tenderness and mercy.

■   *John 13:1-17   (The washing of the feet)*
Jesus sees the ministry of compassion as essentially one of service. Peter, who believes in hierarchy and in power, refuses to allow Jesus wash his feet. But he is told bluntly that unless he is willing to let himself be ministered to, he cannot hope to be of service to others.

■   *Luke 4:1-13   (The temptations in the wilderness)*
We are all tempted to misuse power for our own ends rather than use it for the benefit of others. Jesus refused to abuse his power in any self-serving way. Strength is given to us not for show but for service.

■   *Matthew 18:21-35   (The unforgiving debtor)*
Our natural 'eye-for-an-eye' attitude involves payback for injury and punishment for offence. This parable, however, highlights the importance of forgiveness. We cannot continue to nurse our grievances. We need to let them go.

PRACTICAL SUGGESTION

◊◊◊   *Since we have so much energy at our disposal it can help if we harness this in our prayer. Praying with our body allows us to experience the strength of action and the gentleness of contemplation. Through our body we can move beyond our daily concerns to the deeper realms of the spirit. In particular, we can use the tactile to help us get us experience the divine. Sculpture or pottery, for example, can slow us down and help us get in touch with our deepest energies and feelings. It could also help to surrender ourselves creatively in painting, using colour, line, texture and shape to bridge the gap between our outer and inner worlds.*

NINES

Name It:

My Name:	The Mediator
My Vice:	Sloth
My God:	Ultimate Peace
My Masks:	Indolence, Addiction, Partnership, Union
My Need:	Action
My Virtue:	Diligence

Claim It:

Deep down I'm slothful. That's my brokenness. I don't even bother to try to cover it up. There's no need to, since I have effectively persuaded myself and everybody else that I'm just easy-going. But the truth is that I try to avoid all conflict and am prepared to settle for peace at any price. I don't like to be upset and am always willing to paper over the cracks. To avoid facing problems I tend to sweep them under the carpet, denying that they exist, and make molehills out of mountains to soften the pain. I regularly settle for less.

Basically, I'm cynical about human nature. I see nobody as a big deal, not even myself. I have a poor self-image and am

32

not convinced of my own importance.

The core of my laziness probably lies in my belief that nothing really matters and that, consequently, there's no great harm in taking the path of least resistance. I much prefer to get on with the bits and pieces rather than the things which demand responsibility and commitment. It is hard for me to make decisions and I tend to procrastinate. I regularly put off difficult tasks and become vague or obstinate when people try to pin me down. My lack of response is a form of passive aggression which I find very effective. Because I'm not a self-starter I'm inclined to be addictive. I generally have to look for stimulation outside of myself.

Lord God, I've spent my life trying to deny my feelings. I've attempted to shut them down to avoid the pain they bring. This is how I try to control my environment and gain some power over the ebb and flow of my life. I am 'prone' to inertia, if you'll forgive the pun! I'm afraid of being overwhelmed by uncontrollable emotions. In particular, I swallow my anger and let it fester within. Help me to accept my emotions and allow my gut feelings to surface and give me life.

Tame It:
We try so hard to manage our emotions at every moment that we can miss the beauty, the intensity and the thrill of the present. When we over-value being calm and peaceful the danger is that we find it difficult to become excited or enthusiastic about anything. We have to stop putting ourselves down and continually defining ourselves in terms of what we think others expect of us. Deepening our awareness that we are loved by God precisely for who we are can help us become more self-confident and independent. We will not then feel so overwhelmed by life's difficulties and, instead of withdrawing from the scene, will become actively involved, determine our priorities and accept responsibility for the decisions we make.

The following suggestions for reflection and prayer, though not exhaustive, may help.

■ *John 18: 32-33 (We are not alone)*
Our lack of a real sense of our selves brings with it a deep loneliness. We feel empty inside, as if there is nobody at home. But Jesus reminds us that God's Spirit dwells within each of us. Once we realize that we, too, are important and that we are never alone, we will not be afraid to make the inner jour-

ney to encounter the God in our hearts.

- *John 5:1-16 (Sitting by the pool)*
The sick man at the House of Mercy (Bethesda) spent 38 years at the Sheep Pool waiting for a helping hand. When Jesus saw him there he told him to get up and walk. If we are prepared to seize the opportunities which come our way, we can find healing. On the other hand, if we just sit and wait for something to happen, life may simply pass us by.

- *Luke 8:22-25 (Calming the storm)*
Life is not all plain sailing. It has its inevitable ups and downs. But if we trust in God's providence we will be at peace even in the midst of conflict and turmoil.

- *John 21:1-8 (Throw out the nets)*
Our trust in God's providence can help point us in the right direction. Even when we think our contribution is not worth the effort, God encourages us to make a start. When we are prepared to work with others and do our bit, the results can often surprise us.

- *Matthew 10:28-31   (The hairs on our head are counted)*
Nobody is insignificant in God's sight. We are loved and cared for individually. Recognizing our value and worth is essential to being able to act autonomously. Understanding our dignity leads to greater personal freedom.

PRACTICAL SUGGESTION

◊◊◊ *Since we live in the immediate world of the here-and-now, with all its conflict and all its calm, it can help us greatly to get in touch with the still centre within, where all is gift and harmony. To achieve this we could sit quietly in a church, a prayer room or some other peaceful spot. We don't need to use words, though the 'Jesus Prayer' or a mantra may help give us focus. It is enough to enjoy being in God's presence. We mustn't mistake this for daydreaming or idleness. It is a letting go. The result is often a combination of being sensitively alert while been peacefully serene. When we risk losing ourselves in God, we find God in our deepest selves.*